YANOMAMI

MASTERS OF THE SPIRIT WORLD

PAUL HENLEY

TRIBAL WISDOM

CHRONICLE BOOKS
SAN FRANCISCO

A Labyrinth Book

First published in the United States in 1995 by Chronicle Books.

Copyright © 1995 by Labyrinth Publishing (UK) Ltd.

Design by Generation Associates

The Little Wisdom Library —Tribal Wisdom was produced by Labyrinth Publishing (UK) Ltd.

Printed and bound in Italy by L.E.G.O.

Library of Congress Cataloging-in-Publication Data: Henley, Paul.

Yanomami : masters of the spirit world / by Paul Henley. p. cm.

ISBN 0–8118–0807–6

1. Yanomami Indians.   1. Title

F2520.1.Y3H46 1995

306'.089'982—dc2094-40059

CIP

Distributed in Canada by Raincoast Books,
8680 Cambie Street, Vancouver, B.C. V6P 6M9

10 9 8 7 6 5 4 3 2 1

Chronicle Books

275 Fifth Street, San Francisco, CA 94103

Introduction

uman beings are thought to have inhabited the Amazon Basin for at least ten thousand years before the first Europeans arrived, barely five hundred years ago. The ensuing process of colonization has had the most tragic consequences for the Amerindian inhabitants of Amazonia. An estimated pre-contact population of at least five million has been reduced to less than one million at the present time. Few Amerindian groups have survived this assault on their traditional way of life still intact. Of those that have done so, the Yanomami, who number in the region of twenty-five thousand people, are one of the largest. Their ancestral homeland lies in the Parima Highlands, a rain forest-covered mountain range which divides the tributaries of the upper Orinco from those that flow south toward the mainstream of the Amazon. Today, these highlands also form part of the international boundary between Venezuela and Brazil. About fifteen thousand Yanomami now live in Venezuela and ten thousand in Brazil.

Since the end of the eighteenth century, the Yanomami have been

Page 4: A young Yanomami woman, with the sticks that are worn traditionally as body decoration. *Page 7:* Yanomami warriors find shelter beneath a banana tree leaf. *Page 8:* In the rain forest of Brazil. A Yanomami boy eating a piece of sugar cane. *Opposite:* Fierceness is an important aspect of being a warrior as this young Yanomami man demonstrates.

gradually expanding
out of their homeland,
moving downstream and
thereby coming into closer
contact with the outside
world. Long before they had
direct contact with non-
Indians, they had acquired
certain crops, dogs, and steel
tools by means of trade with
other Indian groups who
acted as intermediaries. But no
Yanomami group had any signif-
icant direct contact with the
outside world until the early part
of this century, and some groups
did not do so until the 1950s. Now
there are very few Yanomami
communities that are not in some
kind of regular contact, direct or
indirect, with the non-Indian
world.

On the basis of certain differences in language and culture, the Yanomami can be divided into four major subgroups: the Sanema, who live farthest to the north; the Yanomamö, who live to the south and west; the Yanomam, who live in the southeast; and the Yanam or Ninam, who live on the eastern side of the territory. The Yanomamö are the largest sub-group, constituting over half the total population. The Yanomam make up almost a quarter of the group and the Sanema somewhat less. The Yanam, the smallest subgroup and the least well known to the outside world, probably number no more than about one thousand people. The Sanema and the Yanomamö communi-ties are mostly located within Venezuela, while the Yanomam for the most part live with-

Above: This Yanomami warrior is shown performing a ceremonial dance. Warfare between communities is becoming rarer as the Yanomami must now battle against the destruction of their forests and way of life. *Opposite:* Decorative arm-band with feathers.

in Brazil. The Yanam are more or less equally divided between the two countries.

As the tide of colonization has reached their territory, the Yanomami have become the victims of age-old stereotypes about Native Amazonians. The popular media of the developed world frequently misrepresent the Yanomami, bestowing on them all the virtues that we lack. Compared with our current preoccupation with the over-exploitation of the natural environment, the Yano-mami are presented as living in perfect equi-librium with nature. Highly romantic images are now commonplace, portraying the Yanomami as childlike, fun-loving innocents living in an earthly paradise.

Unfortunately, this has done very little to halt the continuing invasion of Yanomami land. The situation is particularly serious in the south, within Brazil, where thousands of illegal goldminers are now squat-ting on Yanomami land. The miners' leaders, in concert with the military generals who built the roads that made the invasion possible, have projected a very different image of the Yanomami. They have claimed that as the Yanomami are a backward, violent people, they should be confined to a number of small and scattered reservations, so that others may colonize their land in a (suppos-edly) more productive way.

The accusation of violence made against the Yanomami stems in part from their reputation for fierceness. Among the men of the groups, there is undoubtedly a warrior ethos and one of the most admired manly qualities is to be *waithiri*, translatable as "one who gives as good as he gets." Although fierceness is an important aspect of being *waithiri*, so too are bravery, generosity, and a strong sense of humor, including the ability to laugh at oneself. A man who is *waithiri* will not hesitate to take revenge for a raid on his village. But he will also be generous in distributing food to visitors and relatives on ceremonial occasions.

Under traditional circumstances, warfare is an integral feature of Yanomami life, though it is more frequent in some areas than others. Among the Yanomamö, where the incidence is highest, more than one in four men may die in inter-community raids. But elsewhere it is no more than sporadic. It is also important to set the Yanomamö war deaths in the context of a forty percent mortality rate from epidemic diseases introduced by non-Indians. Under these new threats from the outside, many Yanomami communities have set aside their differences and are no longer actively engaged in raiding one another's villages.

The two contrasting Native Amazonian stereotypes are no more than self-serving misrepresentations: the romantic notion of the "noble savage" is a self-indulgent illusion, while that of the barbarous

savage is merely an excuse for perpetrating outrages against indigenous people. The Yanomami are simply human beings, with all the strengths and weaknesses of the human condition, but also with all the rights. As this book will describe, there are certain aspects of the Yanomami way of life that pose a serious challenge to the values on which modern Western culture is based. But that does not mean that we should not support them in their current struggle to protect their homeland from invasion.

Above: The Yanomami prize generosity above all other qualities. Food is shared amongst relatives.

An Affluent Society

ver innumerable generations, the Yanomami have developed an intimate knowledge of their environment, which enables them to make a good and efficient living from it. On average, they work only two to three days a week on subsistence tasks, yet their diet is as good as that of any rural community outside of the richest parts of the developed world. They prefer to dedicate the rest of their time to feasting, religious ceremonies, or simply lying in their hammocks.

A Yanomami settlement makes an impressive sight from the air, standing out in its clearing amidst the thick forest canopy. Typically it consists of a single large collective dwelling of a roughly conical shape. In the southern settlements, among the Yanomam, this type of house is called a *yano* and is usually inhabited by fifty to eighty closely related people.

A *yano* resembles a vast tepee, with the palm-thatch roof reaching almost down to the ground on all sides. The apex of the structure is left open, leaving a large circular hole for the light to get in and for the smoke from the cooking fires to get out. Inside, there is generally an open-plan arrangement with very few dividing walls. Family hearths are ranged around the perimeter while the central area is used for collective ceremonial purposes.

Farther north, among the Yanomamö, the collective dwelling is known as a *shabono* and tends to accommodate more people, often as many as 150 and frequently more. These houses are also roughly conical in shape, but they may measure as much as a hundred meters across, and the circular opening at the apex is thus very much wider. In fact, a *shabono* no longer looks like a single house, but more like a large circular shelter enclosing a central plaza.

The houses last for about five to seven years, after which time the thatch begins to rot and becomes infested with insects. The group

Previous pages: The Yanomami have a very sound knowledge of their environment, which provides a variety of food sources. This Yanomami woman is laden down by a basket of rain forest fruits.
Above: A *yano*, a Yanomami settlement in Brazil, which may house up to eighty closely related people.

will then generally move off and build a new house elsewhere. In this way, the settlement group also avoids over-exploiting the natural resources in the immediate vicinity.

Yanomami territory extends over roughly sixty thousand square miles, but their population density is very low. Yanomami houses tend to be found in clusters of four or five, separated by no more than a few hours' walk through the forest. Between these clusters, there are large uninhabited areas that are used for hunting and for gathering plants, both of which are essential to the Yanomami diet.

Hunting is the subsistence activity which enjoys the greatest prestige and provides almost all the protein in the Yanomami diet. Only recently, as they have moved down onto major rivers, has fishing assumed any importance. No traditional Yanomami group keeps any domesticated animals except as pets. These they will never eat, even when they belong to an edible species. The Yanomami consider their pets to be similar to human members of the community, and thus to eat them is believed to be tantamount to cannibalism.

Above: Armadillos are hunted by the Yanomami. *Opposite:* Colourful baskets woven by the Yanomami.

Tapir (large, hoofed mammals), peccary (wild pigs), and the giant anteater are the most sought after game, being the largest in the Amazonian rainforest. But the Yanomami also hunt a large number of other species, including deer, capybara (web-footed rodents) and various giant rodents, certain snake species, anteaters, armadillos, tortoises, several species of monkey, and game birds. Some Yanomami groups believe that a hunter will fall sick if he eats his own game. Indeed, if a hunter has been out to hunt with a number of other men, he will not even carry his own meat back to the settlement. This obliges everyone to share out their prey. If a man fails to

do so, he may be deserted by the hawk spirit, which is regarded as essential to the successful hunter.

The Yanomami identify over three hundred different varieties of forest plants. About a fifth of these are useful to them as food, medicine, or for technological purposes. Particularly important to their diet are the many varieties of wild palm fruits which they collect. The Yanomami are also fervent collectors of wild honey and are familiar with fifteen different varieties. Turtles' and birds' eggs, crabs and other crustaceans, spiders, ants, several species of frog, and the larvae of various insect species are all further examples of the wild food resources that play an important part in the Yanomami diet.

However, the main bulk of the Yanomami diet comes from harvesting the gardens which they maintain in the forest just beyond their settlements. These are prepared by cutting down the trees and burning them, thus clearing the undergrowth. The staff of life in most Yanomami communities is the plantain, though they also cultivate a large number of other food plants including manioc, yams, maize, various tropical fruits, and sugar cane. Other important crops are cotton, tobacco, and various medicinal plants.

In Yanomami society, no individual or group can assume permanent ownership of land or any other natural resource. The members of any given settlement may have an informal sense of having a first claim on the game or other forest products nearby. But they will generally have no objection if a friendly neighboring group also uses them for a period. Even this informal claim on local resources is no more than a claim to a right of use. When a settlement group moves off to build a new house elsewhere, the local resources are available to any other group that might subsequently move into the area.

In contrast, there is a strong sense of proprietorship over garden produce.

Accusations of stealing food from gardens are treated very seriously and can often lead to angry disputes both within and between settlements. Even so, one is also expected to share produce from a garden with other members of a settlement. Failure to do so will lead to accusations of stinginess, the most despised of all personal qualities. Yanomami communities are held together by the daily sharing of food, so families who hoard their supplies are a threat to social harmony.

Opposite: Yanomami spend some of their time weaving baskets. This is an example of their handiwork. *Above:* A Yanomami man building the structure for a *yano.*

A Universe of
Many Layers

Previous pages: A Yanomami drawing depicting a hunt.
Above: A palm-thatch roof seen from inside a *yano.*

The Yanomami universe is made up of a series of superimposed layers. The world of the living is called *heika misi*, "this layer." It is thought of as a huge circular disk enclosed by the vault of the sky, in the same way the circular collective house is enclosed by the palm-thatch roof. The sky is called *hedu ka misi*, which may be translated as "the layer of the anaconda." This is a reference to the rainbows that often arch across the sky in Yanomami territory and which remind them of the patterns on the skin of the anaconda. On account of this association, the rainbow is regarded as an ill omen and one which may signal the outbreak of illness.

Above this layer, "on the back of the sky," is the world of the spirits of the dead. This world is very similar to the present one, except that the game is more plentiful and there is no illness. The houses are also much larger because the dead far outnumber the living. Communication between the world of the dead and the world of the living is difficult but not impossible. The spirits of the recently deceased are thought to visit their relatives on earth, and some living shamans claim to have ascended to the world of the dead.

Most Yanomami groups identify another layer above the world of the dead. This is *duku ka misi*, variously translated as a layer that is "luminous," "embryonic" or "newly formed." Some Yanomami groups believe that after an extremely long life, the dead die for a second time and ascend into this highest level of the universe as supernatural winged insects. More commonly, though, this world is considered to be the home of the dangerous and cannibalistic spirits associated with vultures and with the sun and the moon.

The Yanomami also believe in the existence of an underworld. This layer is said to be "rotten," "barren," and above all, "watery." One of the most popular Yanomami myths describes how the culture hero Omamë, hoping to give his son a drink, perforated the ground

with his bow. To his surprise, a great column of water shot up from the underworld and reached the sky, from whence it has been falling ever since as rain.

This underworld is the home of the *amahiri*, degenerate beings who are generally believed to look like Yanomami but who are said by some to be bald and by others to be dwarfs. There is no game in the underworld, nor any gardens, so in order to eat, the *amahiri* come up to this layer and prey upon the souls of living Yanomami, particularly children.

This universe is not unchanging. Some Yanomami groups say that the underworld came about when one of the upper layers crashed against the sun and part of it broke off, carrying the unfortunate *amahiri* with it. The Yanomami have an elaborate account:

The first beings were very ignorant. They didn't conduct funerals properly with the appropriate ceremonial dialogs. Worse, they even used to eat one another. One by one, they metamorphosed into the animals which we hunt today. At that time, one of them who was a great shaman died, and his spirit helpers, furious at being orphaned, set about cutting up the sky with their supernatural weapons. The other shamans tried their utmost to prevent it, but in vain. The ancient sky was so cut up that it collapsed and fell upon the earth. As a result, what was then this layer became the underworld and

Opposite: A Yanomami shaman.
Above: Yanomami stick drawings.

most of the animal ancestors were carried down with it. They became cannibals with long teeth who would henceforth live on the evil spirits sent down to them by shamans. Only a few ancestors managed to escape by taking refuge underneath a giant cocoa tree. Where the sky fell on the tree, it formed a large mountain. Aided by a small parrot with a very sharp beak, they were able to cut their way out.

They discovered that they were standing on "the back of the sky." In effect, the world of the spirits of the dead had now become "this layer." The culture hero Omamë had also come down on "the back of the sky." The spirits of the dead themselves were enclosed like termite eggs within the hollow stem of a palm of the kind from which sorcerers' blow-pipes are made. Omamë heard a rustling noise coming from the stem, so he split it down its length. He extracted the spirits in their termite egg form and deposited them on a leaf. He then transformed them into flesh-and-bone Yanomami and instructed them in the ceremonial dialogs which should be conducted whenever there is a funeral.

Opposite: Elements of the physical world surrounding them are often found in Yanomami mythology. Termites feature prominently in their creation story.   *Right:* After having undergone a rigorous initiation, this young Yanomami shaman is now ready to practice his craft.

Masters of the
Spirit World

lthough most young men aspire to become shamans, not all can withstand the process of initiation, which entails the observance of certain food taboos and other restrictions. The apprentice may not leave the settlement and may eat only roasted plantain or yams. He is not even allowed to drink water; if he is thirsty, he has to quench his thirst with a few pieces of sugar cane. He must constantly walk about in a crouch and must have no contact with women. At night, he must hang his hammock away from the others and is allowed only a small fire to keep out the cold.

During this time, he will consume large quantities of hallucinogenic drugs. The Yanomami prepare several different types of hallucinogens, known generally as *ebene*. The most common variety is *yakowana* which is prepared from the bark of the *Virola elongata* tree. More appreciated but less commonly found is *hisiomö*, or "*yopo*" as it is known in local Spanish, which is prepared from the pulverized seeds of the *Anadenanthera peregrina* tree. The Yanomami also prepare hallucinogenic snuffs from a number of plants which they grow in their gardens but these are less potent and therefore less valued than the wild varieties.

In many Yanomami communities, hallucinogens are routinely taken by most men every day. But for a shamanic initiation, a particularly strong concoction is prepared. One or more varieties of hallucinogenic powder are inserted into a short hollow tube and then blown directly down each of the apprentice's nostrils. His eyes become glazed, he begins to retch and green mucus runs from his nose. But if he has prepared himself properly, he will have visions of paths of light refracting into all the colors of the rainbow. Along these paths, his spirit helpers will come dancing toward him, fluttering and reeling in ecstasy, like a cloud of butterflies.

Previous pages: A Yanomami prepares a fire. *Opposite:* A Yanomami shaman inhaling a hallucinogen that will allow him to contact his spirit helpers.

These shamanic spirit helpers are called *hekura*, and there are thought to be great multitudes of them. Many came into existence when one of the ancestors metamorphosed into animal form. But *hekura* are also thought to be inherent to certain forest plant species as well as to natural phenomena such as whirlpools, the wind, prominent mountains, and certain minerals. The *hekura* represent the vital principle invested in all these life-forms, though there are also some *hekura* which are entirely supernatural without any specific embodiment in the everyday physical world.

Whatever the life-form that they represent, all *hekura* have a human appearance, though they are generally very small, being no more than a few millimeters high. They are said to be exceptionally beautiful and very bright, always decorated with body paint and feathers, as if for a feast. Most *hekura* are male and wear glowing visors around their heads. Some of the plant *hekura* are female and these can be identified by the shining wands protruding from their vaginas. Each *hekura* has the attributes characteristically associated with the life-form it represents and, most importantly, each has its own song.

During an initiation, it is this song that the senior shamans will use to entice the *hekura* down from their lairs in rocky outcrops, under-

neath rapids and waterfalls, or at the point where the vault of the sky meets the earth. The song will usually be accompanied by a dance in which the senior shamans mime the characteristic movements of the life-forms which the *hekura* represent. Their aim is to persuade the *hekura*, one by one, to take up residence in the apprentice's chest. If they are successful, he will thereafter be able to use their attributes in treating the illnesses of his patients.

Opposite: A Yanomami girl, her face decorated with paint and pierced with sticks.
Above: Yanomami warriors dance in the middle of a *yano*.

Casting out Evil

The Yanomami attribute very few illnesses to purely physical causes. They recognize that nowadays many illnesses stem from contact with *nabë*, or non-Indians, and that these are caused by new infections against which they have no natural defense. But under traditional circumstances, the great majority of illnesses are attributed to an attack by supernatural means either on the *në ûtûbï*, the soul essence of the victim, or on that of the victim's *në rishibï*, or animal spirit double.

Supernatural attacks may be carried out either by natural agents or by human beings. The potentially lethal natural agents are evil forest spirits, including the *në ûtûbï* soul essences of certain dangerous animals such as jaguars or vultures. Attacks of human origin may be carried out by enemy shamans with the aid of their *hekura*. Alternatively, they may be perpetrated by means of sorcery involving the use of medicinal plants and other substances.

It is because the victim's *në ûtûbï* has been attacked that the physical body shows signs of illness. Thus in order to bring about a cure, the shaman has to identify the nature of the attack on the soul and then seek to counter it. Only once this has been achieved is there any point in seeking to cure the physical body by medicinal means.

For example, illnesses are often attributed to the effects of a foreign body implanted in the victim's soul by an enemy shaman or by an evil spirit. The shaman performing the cure might then summon the

Previous pages: Yanomami shamans often put themselves in a trance in order to diagnose a person's illness. *Above:* The Yanomami often decorate themselves with body painting for special ceremonial occasions.

hekura of a species of monkey renowned for its climbing ability: its "sticky hands" will enable the shaman to grab the pathogenic object and extract it. Alternatively, he might summon the *hekura* of the anaconda, an animal that often regurgitates its prey before finally consuming it. This regurgitating ability will assist the shaman to vomit up the object which he has sucked out of the patient. Should the patient have a temperature, the *hekura* of a certain species of frog may be invoked to spray cool water over the patient to bring it down.

Shamans render their services to anyone in the community without charge and gain great prestige from doing so. However, it is not only from curing that this prestige is gained: an eminent shaman is also expected to carry out supernatural attacks on enemy communities in revenge for the illnesses which they are thought to have sent in the first place. The reputation of great shamans spreads far and wid throughout Yanomami territory and their power to harm others at great distances is often greatly feared.

=

Life Without

a Trace

=

Funeral feasts, called *reahû*, are the most elaborate of all Yanomami life cycle ceremonies. There are no public celebrations of birth nor of marriage, and initiation into adulthood is a largely private affair. Young girls are required to go into seclusion behind a palm-thatch screen for a few days at the time of their first menstruation. They are said to be in a polluted and vulnerable condition referred to as *unokai* and they have to observe restrictions similar to those of apprentice shamans. In some Yanomami communities, adolescent boys also have to observe these restrictions, though they do not generally go into seclusion. But all of this is relatively minor compared to the *reahû*.

All Yanomami cremate their dead. In some communities, this takes place immediately after a short period of mourning, in the central plaza of the house. But among the Yanomam, the body is first left to rot on a special structure in the forest. After about three weeks, when only the bones remain, these are brought back to the house for cremation. In either case, the cremation itself is only a preliminary event of the *reahû*. The deceased's ashes are carefully transferred to calabashes and stored away while further preparations are made.

The *reahû* proper may not take place for several months. Large quantities of plantains and smoked meat have to be assem-

bled since the event may last for as long as six days. One or more of the neighboring communities will usually be invited and the host community will want to be seen to be generous. The first five days of the ceremony are mostly given over to ceremonial dialogs, food exchanges, and dancing of various kinds. But on the evening of the fifth day, the nearest relative of the deceased will invite one of the visitors to dispose of the

Previous pages: Night falls on the rain forests of Brazil, where many of the Yanomami still live. *Above:* A Yanomami helping during the preparation of a feast.

ashes on the following morning. The exact treatment of the ashes depends on the status of the deceased and the way in which he or she died. Practices also vary from one Yanomami sub-group to another. Amongst the Yano-mamö, the ashes are ritually poured into gourds of plantain soup which are then passed around and solemnly consumed by close kin and friends. If the deceased was killed in warfare, only women will drink the ashes. The ashes of such men will be consumed gradually over the course of many *reahû*, until it is felt that their death has been fully avenged by counter-raids. In this way, it may take as long as ten years for certain individual's ashes to be consumed.

The consumption of a person's ashes is the final stage in a process designed to eliminate all traces of the deceased in the world of the living. Shortly after death, all the deceased's personal possessions are burned and the crops in his or her garden are uprooted. Even the ground where the deceased walked is roughed up to destroy all evidence of his or her footprints. Personal names, which are taboo to utter from adolescence onwards, become even more strictly prohibited.

The intention behind these measures is not simply to avoid painful memories. It is also thought that as long as any personal traces of the dead person still exist in the world of the living, the deceased's soul will be attracted back. This is regarded as extremely dangerous since it may persuade the soul of a living relative to return with it to the land of the dead "on the back of the sky."

Above: A Yanomami woman weaves a basket.

One day a group of souls returned to the shabono where they had once lived. They included the soul of a little girl who had only recently died. The souls discovered that many other inhabitants of the shabono had also died and the shelter was falling down. They therefore set about rebuilding it. The shabono came to life again and everyone was pleased.

The little girl went over to her mother's hearth. She was truly beautiful, and her parents were overjoyed at her unexpected return. She looked just as she did in life, except that her eyes and her nose were aflame.

"Mother, why is the ground dark around our hearth?" she asked.

"Oh, that's just your brother, he's been burning off the grass."

"Mother, why do you have your cheekbones blackened, as if you were in mourning?" she continued.

"Your brother rubbed them with ashes."

"Mother, what have you got in that calabash?"

"Oh, that's just some leaf ash which I use as a condiment," said the mother.

But some parrots that were perched up above blurted out the truth. "They're your own ashes," they said. Just at that moment, a flock of partridges took flight, which is a sign for the souls of the dead to follow them up to the "back of the sky." The mother tried to clasp her daughter to her, but in vain. All she was left with was some burnt pieces of charcoal.

=

A Death for

a Death

=

From an early age, Yanomami children are encouraged to take revenge for any harm that is done to them. Any fatal illness attributed to the work of an enemy shaman demands revenge or else he might strike again. This revenge attack can be carried out through supernatural means by the shamans of the community in which the victim

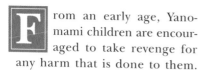

lived. In the past it often took the form of an actual raid by the young warriors.

These raids were frequently plotted with the members of neighboring communities who had been invited to the *reahû* funeral feast of the victim. On the final evening of the feast, the senior shamans would call down the *hekura* of vultures and other birds of prey so that they would be temporarily lodged in the chests of the warriors. Next day, on the way, the warriors would make models of their enemies out of palm leaf bundles and fire arrows at them, imitating the calls of vultures as they did so. But very few of these raids were carried through to the end. At the slightest ill omen, such as an unusual bird call, the raiders would abandon the attempt and return home.

But if the raid actually took place and an enemy was killed, the killer was thought to carry within him the essence of the vulture spirits feasting on the soul of the victim. His breath would stink with the smell of putrefaction and his skin would become greasy with his victim's body fat. All the warriors on the raid would then have to submit to the same food taboos and other restrictions as a young woman undergoing her first menstruation. The same term, *unokai*, was used to refer to both conditions since in each case, the individual who was *unokai* was said to be in a polluted state.

After several days in the *unokai* condition, the warriors would take a plant medicine designed to make them vomit up the last residue of the victim's essence retained within them. They would then bathe in the river and paint their bodies with special designs. This would have had the effect of purifying them and they could have felt satisfied that with his death avenged, the *në borebï* ghost of their relative could leave permanently for the world of the dead. But, meanwhile, the relatives of the newly slain man would already be planning their own revenge.

Previous pages: A Yanomami warrior, adorned with body paint and feathers.
Opposite: A Yanomami man puts the final touches to the feather tip of an arrow.

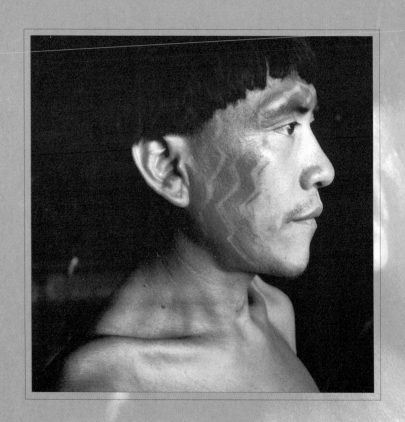

=

*Assault on
the Yanomami*

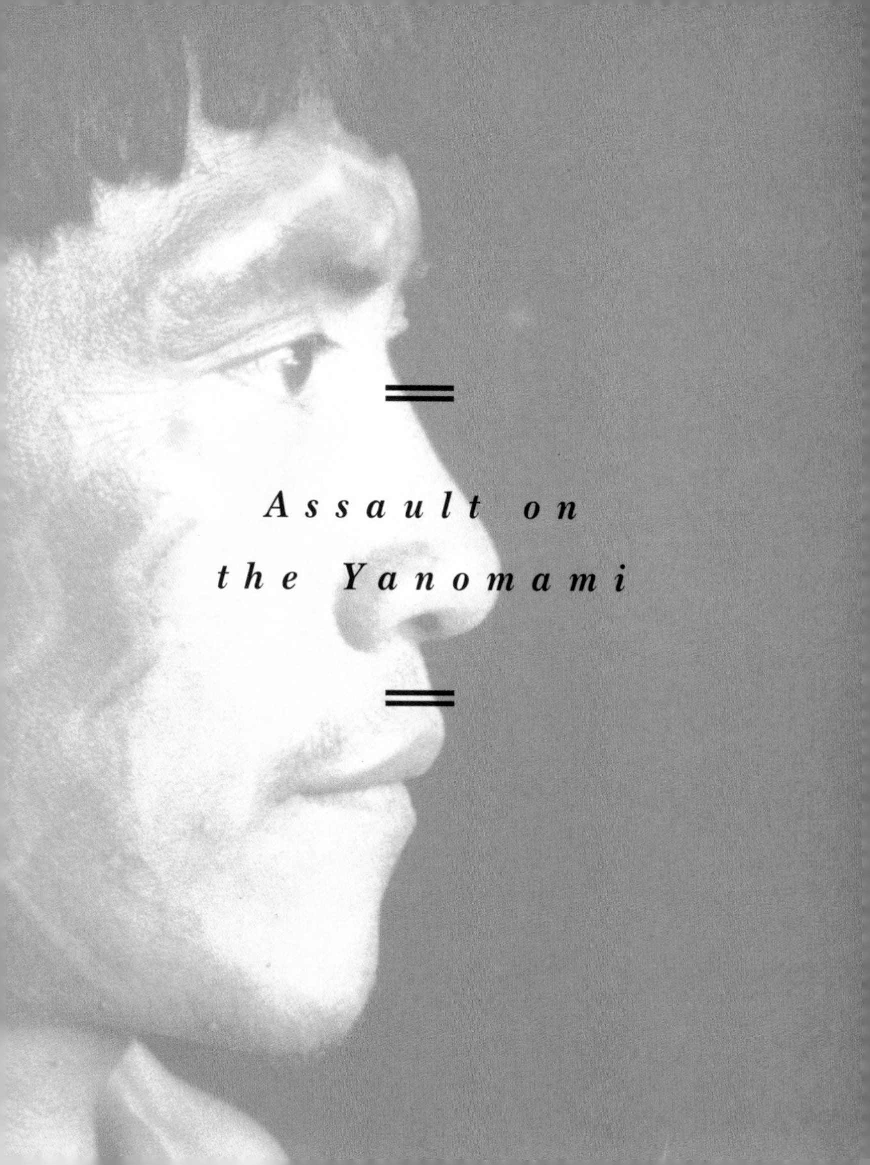

=

The inter-village raiding of the Yanomami pales into insignificance compared to the ongoing assault which they have been suffering in recent years at the hands of illegal small-time miners in Brazil. These invaders have brought diseases such as malaria, tuberculosis, influenza, and other respiratory disorders, against which the Yanomami have no natural defense. The mercury used by the miners has polluted the rivers, and the noise of their machines has scared off the game. Some Yanomami villages have been directly attacked and the inhabitants murdered. The psychological dislocation that this invasion has caused has also been immense.

Survival International, an organization which campaigns for the rights of tribal peoples, estimated

that in a two-year period between 1988 and 1990, as many as 1,500 Yanomami died from diseases or violent confrontation with the miners. This represented about fifteen percent of the total Brazilian Yanomami population. On the Venezuelan side, the invasion of Yanomami territory is not nearly so marked, but there they have also suffered badly from introduced diseases.

Following an international outcry, the Brazilian government issued a decree in 1991 establishing a park covering all Yanomami lands within Brazil. This superseded an earlier plan to confine the Yano-mami to nineteen separate pockets of land that would have excluded approximately seventy percent of their territory. The new decree was a great step forward, but in practice the miners have continued to operate clandestinely in Yanomami territory, and the federal government seems incapable of forcing them to get out. In August 1993, a group of miners attacked the village of Hashimu and killed sixteen Yanomani, mostly women and children. The murderers were never caught.

In the face of this onslaught, the Brazilian Yanomami have set aside

Previous pages: Toto, a Yanomami shaman. *Opposite:* The Yanomami are vulnerable to introduced diseases. Nowadays they often use clinics and Western medical techniques.

their differences and are seeking to resist the invaders. One of their leaders is Davi Kopenawa Yanomami. His words, couched in the language of his ancestors, perceptively link the fate of the world as a whole with that of the Yanomami:

We don't have poor people. Every one of us can use the land, can clear a garden, can hunt, fish. An Indian, when he needs to eat, kills just one or two tapirs.
He only cuts down a few trees to make his garden. He doesn't annihilate the animals and the forest. The whites do this. . .

Omamë hid the shawara diseases under the earth. The miners use machines and dig deep holes in the earth for iron, to make pieces of airplanes, of trains. This stirs up much dust, which the wind carries like smoke, and this makes many people sick...

The whites take oil out of the earth. The oil, the iron, are not dead, they are alive. They only die when they are heated in the factories. Then their spirits go wheeling around through the air, in the wind, and sicken children and old people. The 'shawara' of stones gets out and wants vengeance.

This is the universal sickness of pollution— the disease of smoke. It arises from iron, stones, oil, bombs—all these things. . . . This way everyone will be killed. The world will be destroyed in our own time; it will not survive us.

Opposite: A Yanomami asleep in his hammock.

BIBLIOGRAPHY

The Yanomami are the subject of a vast literature and the information in this book has been distilled from many different sources. One of the most important of these has been the doctoral thesis of **Bruce Albert**, *Temps du sang, temps des cendres: représentation de la maladie, système rituel et espace politique chez les Yanomami du sud-est (Amazonie brésilienne)* presented at Université de Paris X in 1985. Unfortunately, no part of this excellent work has been directly published in English. However some of its insights are incorporated in the book by Robin Hanbury-Tenison cited under "Further Reading," on which M. Albert worked as scientific consultant. Other important sources for the present work include:

Chagnon, Napoleon. *Yanomamö: the Fierce People*. 3rd edition. New York: Holt, Rinehart and Winston, 1983.

Colchester, Marcus. "Myths and legends of the Sanema." *Antropológica*, vol. 56, pp. 25 - 127. Caracas: Fundación La Salle de Ciencias Naturales, 1981.

_____. "The cosmovision of the Venezuelan Sanema." *Antropológica*, vol. 58, pp. 97 - 122. Caracas: Fundación La Salle de Ciencias Naturales, 1982.

Lizot, Jacques. *El Hombre de la Pantorilla Preñada y Otros Mitos Yanomami*. Monografia no. 21. Caracas: Fundación La Salle de Ciencias Naturales, 1975.

_____. "Los Yanomami." In W. Coppens (ed.), *Los Aborigenes de Venezuela*, vol. 3, pp. 479 - 583. Caracas: Fundación La Salle de Ciencias Naturales, 1987.

_____. *Tales of the Yanomami: daily life in the Venezuelan forest*. Canto edition. Maison des Sciences de l'Homme and Cambridge University Press, 1991.

Chagnon, Napoleon. *Studying the Yanomamö.* New York: Holt, Rinehart and Winston, 1974.

Hanbury-Tenison, Robin. *Aborigines of the Amazon Rain Forest: the Yanomami.* Amsterdam: Time-Life Books, 1982.

Lizot, Jacques. *Les Yanômami Centraux.* Cahiers de l'Homme, Nouvelle Série no. 22. Paris: École des Hautes Études en Sciences Sociales, 1984.

Ramos, Alcida. *Categorias etnicas do pensamento Sanuma: contrastes intra-e inter-etnicos.* Trabalhos de Ciencias Sociais, Serie Antropologia, no. 45. Brasilia: Fundaçao Universidade de Brasilia, 1984.

Smole, William. *The Yanoama Indians: a cultural geography.* Texas Pan American Series. Austin: University of Texas Press, 1976.

Taylor, Kenneth. *Sanuma fauna: prohibitions and classifications.* Monografia no. 18. Caracas: Fundación La Salle de Ciencias Naturales, 1974.

Valero, Helena. *Yanoáma: the story of a woman abducted by Brazilian Indians.* As told to Ettore Biocca and translated from the Italian by Dennis Rhodes. London: Allen & Unwin, 1969. Also published in updated and corrected form as, *Yo soy napëyoma: relato de una mujer raptada por los indigenas yanomami,* edited by Emilio Fuentes. Monografia no. 35. Caracas: Fundación La Salle de Ciencias Naturales, 1984.

ACKNOWLEDGMENTS

Every effort has been made to trace all present copyright holders of the material used in this book, whether companies or individuals. Any omission is unintentional, and we will be pleased to correct errors in future editions of this book.

Text Acknowledgments:
The mythological texts reproduced here have been summarized from more than one source. The originals are generally much lengthier and are told, with variations, in many parts of Yanomami territory.
pp. 29-31: Versions of the "Fall of the Sky" are found in Albert (1985), Chagnon (1983) and Lizot (1975).
p.47: Versions of "Return of the Souls" are found in Albert (1985) and Lizot (1975).
p.56: From an interview with Professor Terence Turner, chair of the American Anthropological Association investigative committee into the situation of the Yanomami in Brazil. The full text is reproduced in the *Cultural Survival Quarterly,* Summer 1991, pp. 59-64.

Information on the current situation of the Yanomami in Brazil was derived from the Survival International campaign document, *Yanomami,* which is available from their offices at 11-15 Emerald Street, London WC1N 3QL, England.

Picture Acknowledgments:
Victor Englebert, Surival International: Pages 4, 7, 8, 11, 12, 15, 16, 19, 20, 21, 23, 28, 30, 31, 32, 34, 37, 38, 41, 42, 45, 47, 48, 50, 57, 58.
Peter Frey, Survival International: Pages 22, 36. *Fiona Watson, Survival International:* Pages 46, 52, 54. *Dennison Barwick, Survival International:* Pages 13, 26. *Survival International:* Pages 24, 29.